THE NEW BOOK OF
DINO
S·A·U·R·S

Dr. David Unwin
CONSULTANT – Dr. MICHAEL BENTON

COPPER BEECH BOOKS
BROOKFIELD, CONNECTICUT

Contents

Dinosaurs dominate the science of the 1990s, much as they ruled the world millions of years ago. The pace of research on dinosaurs is greater than ever before and has been fueled by some astonishing new discoveries, such as a dinosaur sitting on a nest of eggs. These and many other new dinosaurs from Africa, Asia, Antarctica, and even the United States are featured in this book. Here you can read for the first time about the largest meat-eating dinosaurs that ever lived, the tracks of huge herds of migrating dinosaurs, nesting dinosaurs, and the latest ideas about why they became extinct.

© Aladdin Books Ltd
1997
*Designed and
produced by*
Aladdin Books Ltd
28 Percy Street
London W1P 0LD

*First published in the
United States in 1997 by*
Copper Beech Books,
an imprint of
The Millbrook Press
2 Old New Milford Road
Brookfield, CT 06804

Printed in Belgium
All rights reserved

Editor Jon Richards
Design
David West
Children's Book Design
Designer Flick Killerby
Illustrators
Richard Rockwood
Rob Shone
James Field (Simon
Girling and Associates)
Picture Research
Brooks Krikler Research

Library of Congress Cataloging-in-Publication Data
Unwin, David. The new book of dinosaurs / by David Unwin ;
illustrated by Richard Rockwood and Rob Shone.
p. cm.
Includes index.
Summary: A look at dinosaurs, including two new giants, Afrovenator
and Carcharodontosaurus, and what they can tell us about our past.
ISBN 0-7613-0568-8 (lib. bdg.). — ISBN 0-7613-0589-0 (pbk.)
1. Dinosaurs—Juvenile literature. [1. Dinosaurs.] I. Rockwood,
Richard, ill. II. Title.
QE862.D5U68 1997
567.9'1—dc20
96-38758
CIP AC

Paleontologists (fossil hunters) will leave no stone unturned and no corner of the world unexplored in their quest for new dinosaur discoveries. Recent expeditions have taken them to some of the least hospitable places on the planet, including the Sahara Desert, Alaska, and Mongolia. Ukhaa Tolgod, in the Mongolian Gobi Desert, has yielded a huge number of dinosaur remains. These animals were all killed and buried where they stood by fierce sandstorms millions of years ago.

Modern technology has come to the aid of the paleontologist. Today, the scientist can use the most powerful electron microscopes to reveal the tiniest details of remains, while high-powered drills and even explosives can expose fossils in even the toughest layers of rock. All of this has greatly expanded our understanding of these amazing animals that mysteriously disappeared about 65 million years ago.

Beginning with a look at the world during the time of the dinosaurs, *The New Book of Dinosaurs* uses amazing computer illustrations to reproduce the very latest discoveries in the world of paleontology. These finds have led scientists to alter their understanding of dinosaurs, from how their bodies worked to how they lived and survived throughout the world. The discovery of new species have also answered some puzzling questions, such as how modern birds evolved.

Dinosaur WORLD

Dinosaurs were the dominant land animals throughout the Jurassic and Cretaceous periods (206-65 million years ago). But their world was very different from ours. Landmasses lay in different positions from today and formed vast supercontinents, such as Gondwanaland and Laurasia (*below*). For long periods of time the continents were connected and dinosaurs could walk to all parts. Early in the Jurassic and again in the Cretaceous sea levels rose and areas of land were flooded by seas, isolating dinosaurs on smaller island continents.

The world was warmer than today and without extreme changes in the seasons. Mild conditions spread to the Poles and there were no ice caps.

THE WORLD OF THE DINOSAUR

Conditions during the time of the dinosaurs were a lot hotter and wetter than they are today. This warm and often humid atmosphere gave rise to lush, dense vegetation (*above*). At ground level there were ferns and in wetter areas, horsetails. Woods and forests were dominated by palm-like cycads, gingkoes, and conifers.

*FLOWERS
Plant communities changed dramatically in the Cretaceous with the appearance of flowering plants (left). These very successful plants soon dominated plant life.*

Dinosaurs shared the plains, forests, and swamps with many other groups of animals. Pterosaurs and primitive birds flew overhead while lizards scampered under their feet (*right*). Turtles, frogs, and crocodiles inhabited lakes, rivers, and marshes and our ancestors, the early mammals, hid in trees or among rocks.

LAURASIA

TETHYS SEA

GONDWANA

SEA LIFE

During the time of the dinosaurs, the seas were dominated by marine reptiles. Ichthyosaurs, the fish lizards, were very similar in size and shape to dolphins and probably fed on fish and squid.

Plesiosaurs, the top predators (*right*), had powerful jaws and rows of sharp, pointed teeth, which they used to kill and tear apart their prey. They were up to 39 feet (12 m) long and had a small head on top of a long, snaking neck.

DRAGONS OF THE AIR

The skies above the dinosaurs' heads were filled with pterosaurs (*left*). With broad, membranous wings and fur-covered bodies, most pterosaurs fed on fish or insects that they caught while flying. Early pterosaurs were about the size of a crow. However, later forms grew very large, reaching giant size with wingspans of 39 feet (12 m), the size of a small airplane.

EARLY MAMMALS

The first mammals evolved from a group of reptiles that existed long before the arrival of the dinosaurs. Early mammals, such as *Megazostrodon* (*right*), were hairy and usually no bigger than a hamster. They did their best to avoid predatory dinosaurs by only coming out at night. With their sharp eyesight and sense of smell, they caught and ate insects, snails, slugs, and other small delicacies.

6

Soft tissue and DNA

Usually only the toughest parts of dinosaurs, their bones and teeth, survive to become fossils. Soft tissues, such as the internal organs, muscles, and skin, decay very quickly or are eaten by predators or scavengers. But sometimes dinosaurs were killed and buried very quickly – some were smothered by huge sandstorms while others fell into dark, poisonous sediments at the bottom of lakes – and parts of their soft tissues were preserved. Skin is the most likely to be found, because it is relatively tough, but remains of muscles have recently been discovered, and some scientists claim to have found blood cells and even fragments of dinosaur DNA.

REAL DNA FROM DINOSAURS?

U.S. researchers claim to have extracted DNA from well-preserved dinosaur bones and Chinese scientists claim to have recovered it from a dinosaur egg. New tests show, however, that it is modern not ancient DNA and probably comes from contamination of the specimens when they were handled by humans. In the film *Jurassic Park* (*left*), scientists brought dinosaurs back to life by growing them from cells into which they had injected dinosaur DNA, extracted from dinosaur blood found in the gut of blood-sucking flies preserved in amber. Theoretically, this technique is possible, but there is less than a chance-in-a-billion that a complete DNA sequence could be found and extracted. The cost of such a technique would be enormous.

Because soft tissues affect the skeleton, paleontologists can use the shapes of bones to try to reconstruct the muscles, guts, and brains. Knobs and crests on limb bones tell us much about the size and position of muscles, internal casts of the braincase reveal the shape of the brain, and the size and shape of the ribs shows how big the guts were.

Girderlike spine supports neck

Entombment in amber is one of the best ways of becoming a fossil. Bones, soft tissues, and stomach contents are preserved in the finest detail. No dinosaurs have ever been found in amber, but lizards, mammals, and insects (*left*) have been.

Insect preserved in amber

If most or all of the skeleton is found, paleontologists are able to reproduce how a dinosaur looked and behaved with a high degree of accuracy. Once the muscles have been placed over the skeleton, the whole animal can be covered in its skin (*right*). Although some skin remains have been found, they only tell paleontologists the skin's texture. For an idea of its color, scientists look to animals that are alive today and have a similar way of life to the dinosaur, i.e. are they hunters or grazers.

Reconstruction of dinosaur muscle

WHAT IS DNA?

DNA (deoxyribonucleic acid) is the recipe that cells use to build living organisms. The DNA is stored in the nucleus which acts as the command center of the cell. Under rare conditions, bits of DNA have been preserved in fossils.

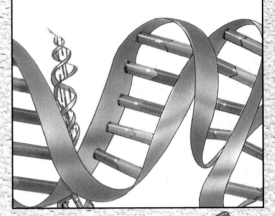

PELECANIMIMUS

Traces of soft tissue around the skull of *Pelecanimimus* (*right*), an unusual new ornithomimosaur found in Spain, show that this small dinosaur seems to have had a small crest on the back of its head and a pouch in the throat region. Perhaps *Pelecanimimus* was a fish-eating dinosaur which grabbed prey using its 200 or so small, sharp teeth, and stored them in the throat sac, much like a pelican does today.

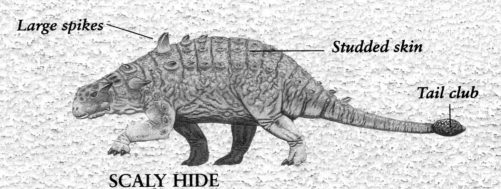

Large spikes

Studded skin

Tail club

SCALY HIDE

Impressions of scaly skin (*left*), much like that of living reptiles, have been found in the fossils of two plant-eating hadrosaurs that died in dry semidesert conditions, and became mummified. The armored skin of four-legged ankylosaurs (*above*) had bony plates and spikes. They also had clubs on the end of their tails, which they could swing violently to defend themselves.

Dinosaur BIOLOGY

Scientists have been arguing about dinosaur biology for more than 150 years. Were they hot- or cold-blooded? Did they grow quickly or slowly? What did they eat and how did they eat it? Over the last decade, new fossils and careful studies of older finds have helped to solve some problems. Most importantly, the structure of the dinosaurs' noses, fine details of their bones, the way they stood, and their distribution show that they were neither hot- nor cold-blooded, but somewhere in between, with a unique type of physiology.

Section through a dinosaur bone, seen through a microscope.

Dinosaur bone

Head and skull of Ceratosaurus

Nose opening

THE NOSE SAYS NO!

Hot-blooded animals breathe relatively quickly, to get air in and out of their lungs. So that they don't lose too much water they have special structures in the nose that help to trap moisture as the air is breathed out. Scientists have been looking up dinosaurs' noses, such as *Ceratosaurus* (*above*), to see if they had these moisture traps, but none have been found so far, indicating that dinosaurs were not hot-blooded.

Under the microscope, thin sections of dinosaur bone can show very fine details. The South African paleontologist Anusuya Chinsamy recently discovered that many dinosaur bones contain bands – a bit like tree rings (*left*) – and used this to calculate how fast dinosaurs grew. She found that the theropod *Syntarsus* (*below*) took 7 years to reach 44 pounds (20 kg) and the early sauropod *Massospondylus* (*right*) 15 years to grow to 550 pounds (250 kg). This is much slower than modern mammals of the same size.

Syntarsus

DINO DUNG

Fossilized dinosaur dung has been known for many years, but, not surprisingly, has been largely ignored. Scientist Karen Chin has made a detailed study of dinosaur droppings and found that coprolites (pieces of fossilized dung) of the hadrosaur *Maiasaura* contain bits of conifer twigs and tunnels made by dung beetles (*below*). So it would seem that dung beetles have been around for at least 80 million years.

FIGHT TO THE DEATH

At first, the skeleton of a theropod, *Velociraptor*, found together with the skeleton of a *Protoceratops* (*left*), a sheep-sized herbivore, was thought to be that one-in-a-million fossil – a predator preserved in the act of capturing its prey. However, some paleontologists have argued that the skeletons were accidentally buried together. A fresh study of the remains (*below*) has proved that the two were actually fighting; clawing and biting each other only to be killed and buried by a violent sandstorm.

Skull of Diplodocus

Fighting Velociraptor *and* Protoceratops

Scientists have often wondered how sauropods (huge, four-legged plant eaters) could eat enough to feed themselves. New studies of their teeth show that some sauropods, such as *Diplodocus*, could strip branches in seconds by raking the foliage through their teeth (*right*). This unusual method of feeding is revealed by wear marks on the surface of the teeth.

Feeding Diplodocus

Massospondylus

Dinosaur TRACKS

In recent years, there has been a great upsurge of interest in dinosaur tracks. These tracks are very important because they provide the only direct evidence of how dinosaurs lived. From tracks we can tell how dinosaurs stood, how they moved, how fast they could run, and whether they lived in herds or on their own.

Many tracks show that some dinosaurs, such as sauropods and ornithopods, lived in herds. Lots of tracks heading in the same direction, equally spaced out and all bending at the same time, show that they were made by a herd passing by, and not lots of single animals over a long period of time.

Dinosaur footprint

Dinosaur tracks

Dinosaur trackers working in North America have found huge numbers of tracks made in the same 100-million-year-old coastal plain sediments. These run north to south for about 40 miles (65 km). This megatrack site, named the Dinosaur Freeway, may have been used as a migration route (*right*).

PTEROSAUR TRACKS

Since the late 1970s, there has been a furious debate about how pterosaurs moved on the ground. New, well-preserved tracks, found in both the United States and France in the early 1990s, show that these batlike creatures were flat-footed and walked on all fours (*below*).

DEATH BY DINOSAUR

Life was dangerous in the time of the dinosaurs. Even if you were not caught and eaten, you could be crushed to death. This is what happened to a group of shellfish, trampled to death by a sauropod paddling along in a shallow lake in Colorado 150 million years ago.

MARTIN LOCKLEY

Discoverer of many important dinosaur tracks and author of numerous articles and books on dinosaur tracking, Martin Lockley, a British paleontologist who lives and works in Colorado, has rescued paleoichnology (the study of fossil tracks) from its backwater status and propelled it into the mainstream of paleontological research.

In his career Martin Lockley has described many important new finds including the prints of *Tyrannosaurus*, the tracks of pterosaurs, and the Dinosaur Freeway (*see left*).

STAND UP STRAIGHT

Paleontologists have long argued whether ceratopsians like *Triceratops* had upright forelimbs, or whether they stuck out to the side, like lizards. Tracks made by *Triceratops* and recently found in rocks near Denver, Colorado, show that ceratopsians stood upright when they walked (*left*).

Tracks have shown some unusual features of dinosaur behavior. In one example (*above*), one of the toes from the left foot of a therapod was missing. The tracks also show that the dinosaur walked with a limp, as shown by the short, irregular steps it made.

Polar DINOS

During the last ten years, dinosaurs have been collected from the North Slope of Alaska, and new finds have been made in Australia, New Zealand, and Antarctica (red dots *above right*). These discoveries show that dinosaurs often lived close to, or even in the polar regions. This is very surprising, as modern reptiles, such as snakes and crocodiles, can only live in warm and temperate regions of the Earth. So how did the dinosaurs manage to live in polar conditions, where modern animals and even humans find it difficult to survive?

Hypsilophodon

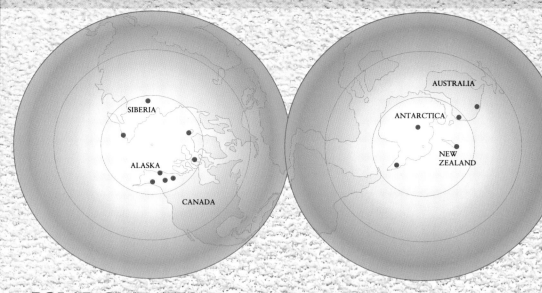

POLAR CLIMATES

During the time of the dinosaurs, the world was warmer (*see pages 4-5*). New studies of plant fossils show that the average polar temperature may have been as high as 46°F (8°C) and periods of freezing, if they took place, were probably short lived. However, there was another problem – dinosaurs living in polar regions would have had to endure long periods of darkness that lasted for up to six months.

Excavating at Dinosaur Cove

Found in 1983, Dinosaur Cove near Melbourne, Australia, has the world's only dinosaur mine. Along with hypsilophodontid dinosaurs, such as *Leaellynasaura* (*see right*), it has produced remains of a pterosaur and a plesiosaur. The rock containing the fossils is very hard and explosives and drills have to be used (*left*).

Cryolophosaurus

SEEING IN THE DARK

Leaellynasaura (*below*), a chicken-sized hypsilophodont found at Dinosaur Cove in Australia, had large eyes and a well developed brain. With its sharp eyesight, this nimble two-legged plant-eater may have been able to remain active throughout the darkness of the long, gloomy polar winter nights.

Leaellynasaura

In the early 1990s, a team of American geologists found the remains of more than three dinosaurs at a site in the Central Transantarctic Mountains, near the South Pole (*above*). The most important find is *Cryolophosaurus*, a rather peculiar theropod that was 26 feet (8 m) long and had short horns above its eyes and a strange crest on the top of its head (*left*).

HIBERNATION

Dinosaurs could also have avoided the dark period by hibernating (*below*). By "shutting down" their bodies and allowing their temperatures to fall close to freezing, dinosaurs might have been able to survive long periods of cold and dark.

MIGRATION

Hibernating dinosaur

Perhaps dinosaurs avoided the long periods of darkness by migrating with the sun, moving toward the Poles in the spring and away from them in autumn. Large herbivorous dinosaurs, such as *Edmontosaurus* (*below*), a hadrosaur that lived in Canada, may have migrated up to 1,250 miles (2,000 km).

Edmontosaurus

Nesting DINOS

Paleontologists have long known that dinosaurs laid their eggs in nests, and thought that, like other reptiles, they left their young to hatch out on their own and fend for themselves. But, an astonishing discovery made in the Gobi desert in 1993 shows that some may have sat on the nest. A complete skeleton of *Oviraptor*, with its legs tucked beneath it and arms curled around its sides had been buried in a sandstorm while sitting on a nest of 22 eggs.

Egg of therizinosaur

NESTING GROUNDS

Dinosaur nesting grounds containing lots of closely spaced nests that seem to have been used year after year were first reported in the 1980s. New discoveries in Mongolia show that, sometimes, different kinds of dinosaurs nested together. Indian paleontologists have just discovered a dinosaur hatchery that contains the fossilized eggs of titanosaurs (large sauropods) and might be 600 miles (960 km) long.

Clutches of dinosaur eggs were laid in many different ways: Most were laid in circles (above), but some were laid in rows, either in arcs or in straight lines.

The discovery of an Oviraptor *sitting on a nest of eggs (right) has altered paleontologists' view of the role of dinosaur parents. They now appear to have cared for their young until they were quite developed.*

Huge numbers of dinosaur eggs have recently been found in cretaceous rocks in central China (*right*). Among these are the largest eggs ever found and the eggs of therizinosaurs containing complete and beautifully preserved embryos at various stages of development. It is very rare for dinosaur embryos to stay this intact.

Chinese dinosaur eggs

EMBRYOS

Embryos are very rare, but sometimes, as in the case of this *Oviraptor* embryo (*left* and *below*) discovered in Mongolia, they are found still in the egg. Not only does this tell us what dinosaur embryos looked like, it also tells us which kind of dinosaur laid the egg!

Oviraptor *embryo in the egg*

EGG THIEF

Oviraptor (*above*) was long thought to be an egg-thief that gobbled up the eggs of *Protoceratops*, a small sheep-sized ceratopsian (*see page 22*). It was believed that *Oviraptor* would crush eggs between its large, curved, horny jaws. In fact, it was a dutiful parent staying with its unborn young even to the point of death.

Tiny, fragile bones of baby pterosaurs were recently found by Russian paleontologists in sands laid down in an estuary in central Asia some 80 million years ago. The babies, which must have been looked after by their parents (*right*), probably fell from nests built in large plantain trees bordering the estuary.

Mother and baby pterosaur

Like modern-day birds, baby dinosaurs may well have used egg teeth to chip their way out of the egg (*above*). After a while, this egg tooth may have fallen off. The young dinosaur may also have been helped out of the egg by the parent. Alternatively, the egg may not have had a tough shell, but, like the egg of a turtle, may have been quite leathery and relatively easy to hatch out of.

T. rex

For many, *Tyrannosaurus rex* is symbolic of dinosaurs as big, fierce, and extinct. But we know surprisingly little about *T. rex*. It is only in the last few years that complete skeletons with skulls have been found. Much work remains to be done on these before *T. rex* gives up all its secrets.

For many years, *T. rex* was thought to have stood and walked in an upright position, but new models based on studies of well-preserved fossils show a much more aggressive, agile-looking animal with its head thrusting forward and a long, stiff tail counterbalancing it behind.

At 40 feet (12 m) long and a weight of at least 6 tons T. rex was one of the largest land predators of all time.

In modern crocodiles, the first chevron, a bony spike found under the tail vertebrae is smaller and farther from the pelvis in females, than in males, probably to leave more room for eggs to pass. Exactly the same situation has been found in skeletons of *T. rex* (*right*).

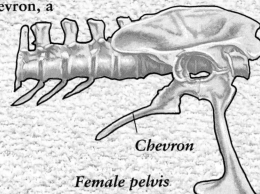

Chevron

Female pelvis

BITTEN BY A REX

Deep bite marks in the bones of a *Triceratops*, found in Montana in 1995, match the shape of *Tyrannosaurus'* teeth (*left*) and show that this dinosaur had been chomped on by *T. rex*.

Forelimb

Hindlimb

The massive mouth (*left*) and huge jaw muscles gave *T. rex* an immensely powerful bite. It would have been able to chomp a human in half with one snap of its jaws. Strong wear patterns on their teeth show that tyrannosaurs regularly chewed up flesh and bones. Scars on their skulls also show that they often fought each other.

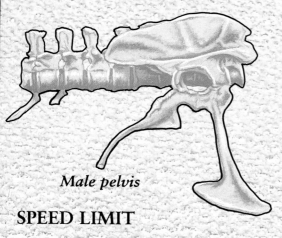

Male pelvis

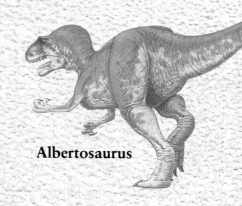

Albertosaurus

Close relatives of T. rex include *Albertosaurus, Daspletosaurus,* and *Tarbosaurus*. All lived at about the same time as *Tyrannosaurus*, in the same region and were about the same size and shape. A new relative, *Siamotyrannus* (*below*), was found in Thailand in 1993. A lot smaller than *Tyrannosaurus* and at least 30 million years older, it gives us some idea of what T. rex's ancestors looked like.

SPEED LIMIT

New studies on the design of the skeleton of *Tyrannosaurus* have found that this dinosaur (*below*) was so heavy that it would be badly hurt or possibly killed if it fell over while running at more than 20 mph (32 km/h). But *Tyrannosaurus rex* didn't need to run fast – there was nothing to run from and prey could always be ambushed and killed with a single bite.

Counterbalancing tail

Siamotyrannus pelvis

WHO OWNS SUE?

Sue, discovered in South Dakota in 1990 by Susan Hendrickson, is one of the most complete and best preserved examples of *T. rex* (*below*). Unfortunately, there is a dispute over who owns Sue: the people who found her; the man who sold it to them; or the Sioux Indians who own the land? Until this is sorted out, Sue is being held "under arrest" by the FBI in Rapid City, South Dakota.

A new study by the American paleontologist Tom Holtz confirms ideas that *T. rex* is more closely related to coelurosaurs (small, lightly built two-legged hunters) than any other dinosaurs. A vital clue comes from the shape of the foot bones (*left*). In both the feet of *Tyrannosaurus* and the coelurosaurs, the middle bone of the three toes is pinched slightly at the top (left). This shows that *Tyrannosaurus* was a super-heavyweight coelurosaur.

Pinched foot bone

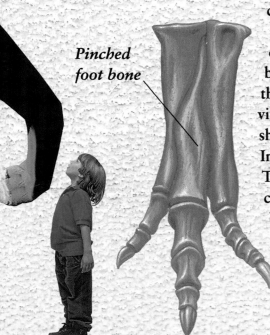

Foot of T. rex

Theropod PREDATORS

Two-legged theropods, including *T. rex*, were some of the largest and most ferocious predators of the Dinosaur Age. Newly discovered remains of one, *Carcharodontosaurus*, including an almost complete skull, reveal the huge size of this African dinosaur. Found in 1995 by an American expedition to the Atlas Mountains in Africa, this dinosaur had a skull that was 5 feet (1.6 m) long (*below*) and may have been even larger than than *T. rex*. *Carcharodontosaurus* was a frightful predator, capable of killing and consuming other large animals. It shared its habitat with *Deltadromeus*, a smaller predator (*right*).

Eoraptor

EORAPTOR

Dinosaurs were just appearing 230 million years ago. One of the first was *Eoraptor* (*above*), found by Paul Sereno in Argentina. This small, lightly-built dinosaur was only about 3 feet (1 m) long. It was certainly one of the earliest and most primitive theropods known and might even be closely related to the ancestor of all dinosaurs.

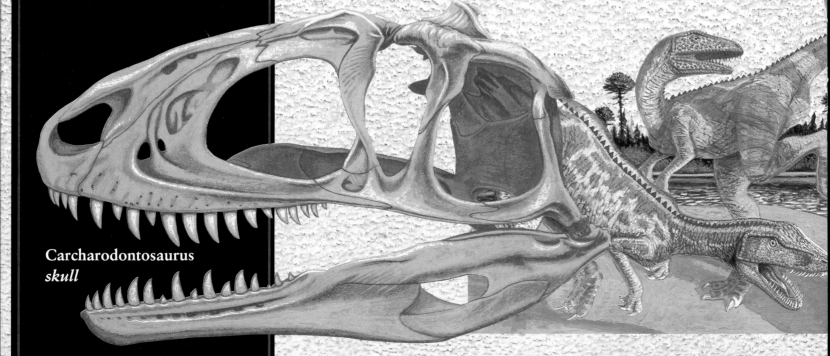

Carcharodontosaurus *guards its kill against a pair of* Deltadromeuses.

Carcharodontosaurus *skull*

Giganotosaurus

The theropod *Giganotosaurus* (*left*) lived about 100 million years ago and may have been the largest land predator ever.

The skull is about the same size as that of *Tyrannosaurus*, but its leg bones are a little longer and sturdier, suggesting that this animal was heavier and even more massive than *Tyrannosaurus*.

AFROVENATOR

In 1993, an expedition to Niger, Africa (*left*), led to the discovery of *Afrovenator* (*below*), a large predatory dinosaur that was 30 feet (9 m) long.

Afrovenator

Between 1986 and 1990 joint Chinese-Canadian expeditions to northern and western China found large numbers of new fossils including Sinraptor, Monolophosaurus, *and* Sinornithoides. *Many of these new specimens are now on view in Chinese museums* (above).

BARYONYX

Finding a skeleton is only the first step in a long task of collecting a new dinosaur. It took more than ten years for the staff at the Natural History Museum in London, England, to free the bones of *Baryonyx*, a predator, from the rock in which it was buried 120 million years ago (*below*).

Alxasaurus MYSTERY

Ever since the 1950s, paleontologists in central Asia have been finding odd pieces of some very peculiar, large, long-armed dinosaurs from the Cretaceous era. The first bones to be found were thought to be those of turtles, and even when they were identified as a dinosaur, no one could agree as to what kind of dinosaur it was.

The discovery of a nearly complete skeleton of *Alxasaurus* (*main picture*) has cleared away much of the mystery. *Alxasaurus* is a therizinosaur and shows that lots of other odd dinosaurs belong to this group. But what did therizinosaurs use their peculiar teeth, long arms, and huge claws for?

Alxasaurus *eating gingko leaves next to a* Psittacosaurus.

LIFE STYLE

The odd shape of *Alxasaurus'* teeth (*see right*) suggests that it fed on plants, such as the leaves from ginko trees (*below*). Sitting or squatting on its haunches, *Alxasaurus* dragged branches and fronds toward its mouth using its powerful arms and long claws (*bottom left*). Alternatively, by rearing up on its hind limbs and supporting itself with its forelimbs, *Alxasaurus* could reach up with its long flexible neck to strip leaves from the tops of small trees.

*Gingkoes (*left*) are one of the few remaining examples of non-flowering plant groups known as gymnosperms. The Gingko tree was once abundant in the time of the dinosaurs but is now only found wild in China.*

HABITAT

Fossils collected from the sediments in which the bones of *Alxasaurus* were preserved show that this animal lived in a well-vegetated river valley, which included conifers, ferns, and flowering plants. *Alxasaurus* shared this environment with turtles, the crocodilelike champsosaurs, and *Psittacosaurus*, a small, bipedal, plant-eating dinosaur (*below*).

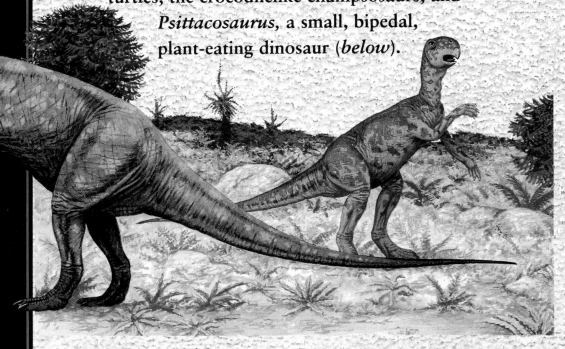

WHOSE RELATIVES?

Therizinosaurs have such a peculiar body that it has been very difficult to find out which major group of dinosaurs they might belong to. Some paleontologists put them in a separate group all of their own, some thought that they might be related to sauropods, while others put them in the middle between sauropods and theropods. However, newly discovered remains show that they are theropods.

SKULLS AND TEETH

The preserved skull of *Erlikosaurus* is the best evidence we have to tell us what the head of therizinosaurs looked like. The skull was small compared to the rest of the animal, the eyes were large, and the snout was long. The teeth were small and pointed and not like the dagger-shaped teeth of typical flesh-eating dinosaurs.

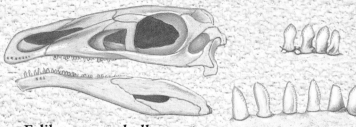

Erlikosaurus *skull*

E ach of the three fingers of therizinosaurs bore a huge claw. The claw (*below*) was long and narrow, but straight rather than hooked as it is in flesh-eating dinosaurs.

Alxasaurus *claw*

T he arms of *Alxasaurus* are quite long, while those of *Therizinosaurus*, its larger descendant, are extraordinarily large and perhaps longer even than the hindlimbs. The upper arm bone, the humerus, bears an enormous bony crest for the attachment of a huge chest, or pectoral muscles, and shows that therizinosaurs had extremely powerful arms.

The hips of therizinosaurs are massive and the legs relatively short and sturdy (right). The feet are quite broad and therizinosaurs probably walked in a flat-footed fashion rather than running on their toes.

Horned DINOS

Ceratops, the "horn-faced" dinosaurs, were so common throughout the Late Cretaceous that they have been called the sheep of the Dinosaur Age. Early forms such as *Protoceratops* were not much larger than sheep, while later ceratops such as *Triceratops* were often as big as a rhinoceros, or even larger. These plant-eaters had strange crests and horns around the skull and parrotlike beaks that were used to chomp up tough plant material. Even though many ceratops have already been unearthed and described, new ones including *Einiosaurus*, discovered recently in Montana, continue to be found.

Immense bone beds consisting of the jumbled up skeletons of hundreds and sometimes thousands of ceratops have been found in North America. It seems likely that these animals were killed by a catastrophe, such as a huge flood.

FEEDING

Ceratops had a toothless beak which they used to bite off plant twigs and leaves. Tougher material was sliced up in a scissorlike fashion by teeth at the back of the mouth *(left)*.

Ceratops *teeth*

HORNS AND FRILLS
Ceratops are distinguished by an astonishing variety of horns as well as a selection of frills that were also edged in horns (below). The full display was only developed when they reached full adulthood.

Chasmosaurus

Styracosaurus

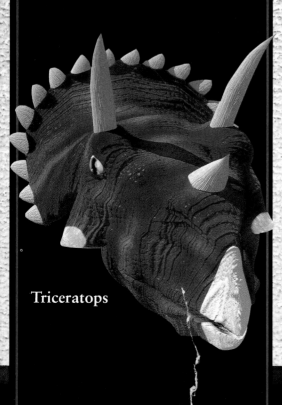

Triceratops

Ceratops were almost certainly preyed upon by theropod hunters (*see page 9*). If they were threatened by a predator, herds of *Einiosaurus* could protect their young by bunching together with the adults facing out on the outside (*below*). This is similar to the behavior of modern-day Musk Oxen from the Arctic.

WHAT'S IN A NAME

Each species of dinosaur has a scientific name composed of two words, written in Latin or Greek. The name usually describes a predominant feature of the animal. For example, *Einiosaurus procurvicornis* means "buffalo lizard with a forward-curving horn."

Young Psittacosaurus *skulls*

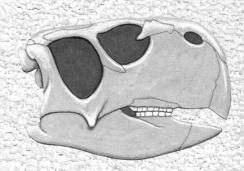

YOUNGSTERS

In some dinosaurs, such as *Psittacosaurus*, an early ceratops, there are fossil remains for all stages of growth from the very young to the fully-grown adult (*above*). Like human babies, young dinosaurs had skulls with large eyes and separate bones to allow for lots of growth. These separate bones would fuse together to form a single skull in later life (*left*).

It seems likely that the horns were used for display purposes and also for fighting. This points to the existence of hierarchies within herds. The horns may have been used to gouge and stab attacking animals or even other members of the same herd. They may even have become interlocked (*right*), as can happen with the horns of modern antelope and deer.

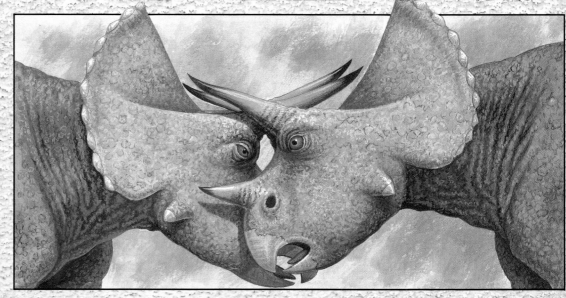

Giant Dinos

There is probably a limit to the size to which animals can grow and it seems likely that sauropods got close to that limit. *Seismosaurus*, from the Late Jurassic and found in New Mexico, was about 150 feet (46 m) from nose to tail. It was probably the longest sauropod. *Ultrasauros*, found in Utah, was 50 feet (15 m) or more in height and was certainly the tallest. In terms of sheer size, however, a recent discovery from Argentina, *Argentinosaurus* currently holds the record for the biggest dinosaur, with an estimated weight of up to 100 tons. It takes time to grow to such a large size and animals such as these probably lived for 50 to 100 years or perhaps even centuries!

LATEST FINDS

The latest discoveries of sauropods come from Madagascar. The most important find is an almost complete titanosaur. So far fossils of this important but poorly known group of Late Cretaceous sauropods have been very fragmentary.

Ultrasauros
This huge plant-eater (right) was more than 82 feet (25 m) long and weighed up to 50 tons. In relation to the rest of its body, it had a small head that sat on top of a towering giraffelike neck.

Supersaurus
Weighing about the same as Ultrasauros (see left), this dinosaur (below) had a neck that was 32 feet (12 m) long, allowing it to pick leaves from very tall trees.

SAUROPODS GET A GRIP

The hand of sauropods had a claw on the thumb. Scientists have often wondered what its function was. New findings show that it was probably used to grip trees as they stood on hind limbs to reach high into the foliage for the most succulent leaves (*right*).

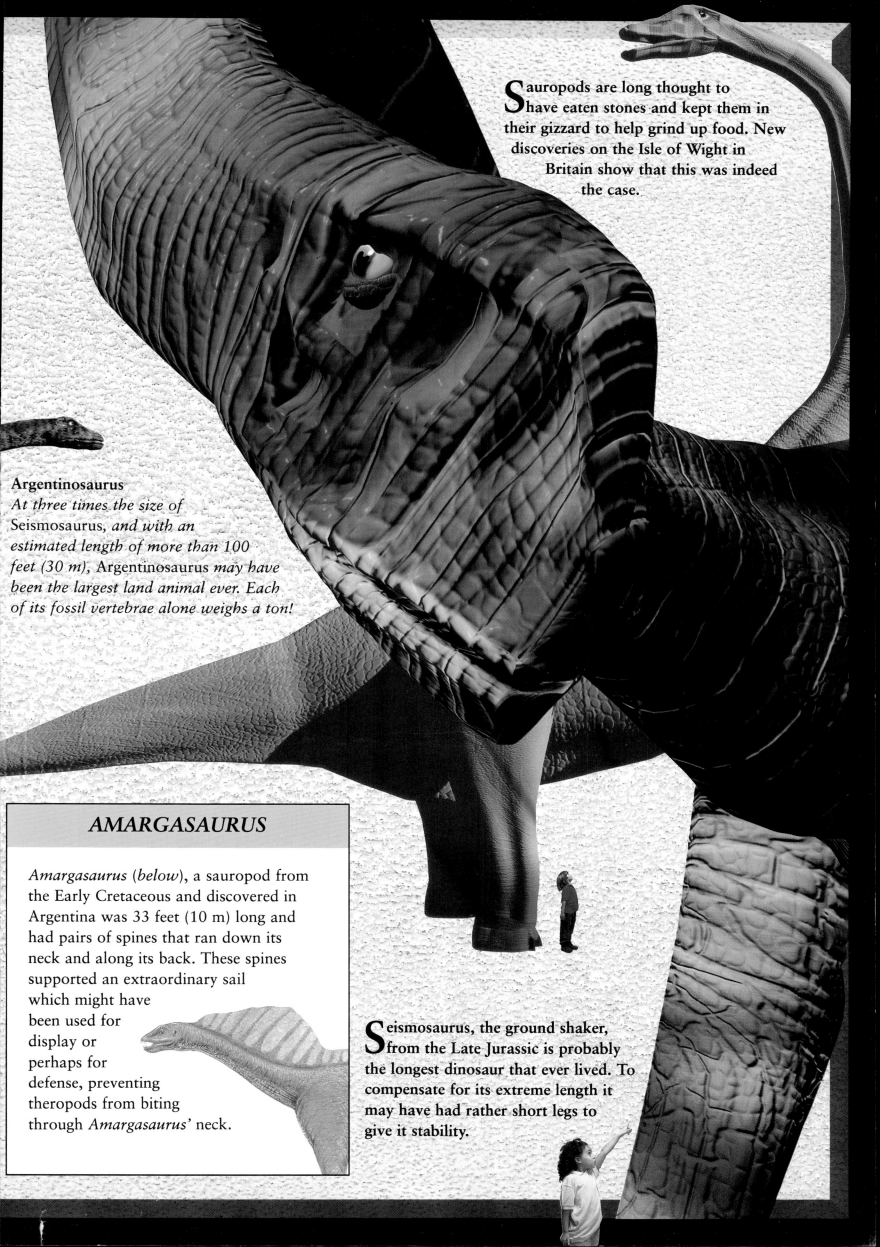

Sauropods are long thought to have eaten stones and kept them in their gizzard to help grind up food. New discoveries on the Isle of Wight in Britain show that this was indeed the case.

Argentinosaurus
At three times the size of Seismosaurus, and with an estimated length of more than 100 feet (30 m), Argentinosaurus may have been the largest land animal ever. Each of its fossil vertebrae alone weighs a ton!

AMARGASAURUS

Amargasaurus (*below*), a sauropod from the Early Cretaceous and discovered in Argentina was 33 feet (10 m) long and had pairs of spines that ran down its neck and along its back. These spines supported an extraordinary sail which might have been used for display or perhaps for defense, preventing theropods from biting through *Amargasaurus'* neck.

Seismosaurus, the ground shaker, from the Late Jurassic is probably the longest dinosaur that ever lived. To compensate for its extreme length it may have had rather short legs to give it stability.

Birds that FILL the GAP

Archaeopteryx, the most primitive known bird (pterosaurs were not birds), has lots of dinosaur characteristics and shows that birds evolved from theropods *(see pages 18-19)*. Until recently, *Archaeopteryx* and one or two other species, such as *Hesperornis*, were the only known birds from the age of the dinosaurs. There was little evidence indicating exactly when and how birds evolved. Fortunately, the last ten years have seen some spectacular discoveries. These include fossils from China with feathers preserved intact *(below)*, and the dinosaurlike bird *Mononykus (right)* found in Mongolia. These show how the bird wing evolved and how other important features such as perching developed.

FLOCK OF BIRDS FROM SPAIN

Important discoveries of early birds have recently been made in Spain. The skeletons of *Nogueornis* and *Concornis* have features which show that although these birds were around only a few million years after *Archaeopteryx*, they had well-developed wings and were strong fliers. Special adaptations in the foot also allowed them to perch on branches like modern birds.

Skeleton of Protoavis

Skeleton of Mononykus

Called *Mononykus (left)*, this animal from the Late Cretaceous, was about the size of a turkey. It had a skull very similar to a bird's, but a pelvis not unlike that of a dinosaur. The most distinctive features were its short, stubby forelimbs, each with a single claw. Scientists cannot agree whether this was a flightless bird or a peculiar burrowing dinosaur that used its forelimbs to dig into the ground.

ARCHAEOPTERYX

The relationship between dinosaurs and modern birds first came to light with the discovery of a feathered dinosaur in 1861. This animal was named *Archaeopteryx* ("ancient wing" – *right* and *below*), and was clearly an early bird but it had one or two strange features. Although the head is fairly birdlike, its jaw was lined with small teeth, whereas birds have beaks or bills. *Archaeopteryx* also had a long bony tail with feathers growing along it. In contrast, modern birds' tail feathers all grow from the base of a stubby tail.

Fossil remains of Archaeopteryx

The discovery of *Protoavis* (*left*) was probably the most controversial find of the last decade. Some paleontologists argue that *Protoavis* was a bird. If this is true, then birds must have first appeared more than 50 million years earlier than *Archaeopteryx*!

AGE OF THE BIRDS

The diagram (*below*) shows when various birds lived. The examples include *Archaeopteryx* (1), *Mononykus* (2), Enantiornithines (3), *Patagopteryx* (4), Hesperornithiforms (5), Ichthyornithiforms (6), and modern birds (7).

CONFUCIUSORNIS

In the last few years many examples of *Confuciusornis* (*right*) have been found in China dating from the Early Cretaceous. It was well-designed for tree climbing but its wings were far too short to make *Confuciusornis* a very good flier.

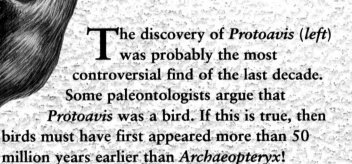
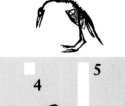

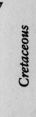

3 4 5 7

2

6

1

Cretaceous

Jurassic

Extinction THEORIES

Death is inevitable for all individuals, and species are always disappearing – this is called background extinction. Sometimes, entire groups can disappear. This occurred at the end of the Cretaceous (65 million years ago), when the dinosaurs died out, along with many other types of animal and plant life. Such events are called mass extinctions. As well as being bad news for some groups, it can be good news for others, allowing them to arise from obscurity and take over new habitats. Many theories exist as to what

caused mass extinctions. These can range from the serious, such as volcanic activity and a meteorite impact, to the bizarre, such as a space-borne plague or even alien hunters!

VOLCANIC ERUPTIONS

Huge volcanic eruptions (*above*) are known to have taken place at the same time as mass extinctions, including the one at the end of the Cretaceous. These eruptions may have led to acid rain on a global scale, a mini-ice age, and then an abrupt swing into a greenhouse type climate. This could have killed off the dinosaurs.

Many other groups including the pterosaurs, marine reptiles, such as plesiosaurs and mosasaurs (*see page 5*), other forms of oceanic life, which include the ammonites (*right*), and some kinds of plants all died out together with the dinosaurs.

TARGET EARTH

The impact of a large meteorite may have caused a global catastrophe big enough to wipe out the dinosaurs. But where's the crater? A huge bowl-shaped structure more than 113 miles (180 km) across has been found near Chixulub (the "Devil's Tail") (*right*) in Mexico. It was formed 65 million years ago, exactly when the dinosaurs died out!

Mexico

Meteorite impacts are very common – the Earth is constantly being hit by small bits of debris from space. However, large impacts occur less frequently. Meteor Crater in Arizona (*left*) was caused by a meteor that hit the Earth only 50,000 years ago.

A mass extinction at the end of the Triassic may have allowed the dinosaurs to rise to prominence, while another at the end of the Cretaceous finished off the dinosaurs and gave mammals their chance to evolve (below).

ARE THEY EXTINCT?

In many ways, it can be said that not all of the dinosaurs were killed off by the mysterious mass extinction 65 million years ago. Their descendants, the birds, can be found on every continent of the world. These successful animals range in size from tiny hummingbirds to eagles, penguins, and enormous ostriches (*below*).

Glossary

Ammonites
Coiled shellfish that are closely related to squid and octopus. They died out at the end of the Cretaceous Period.

Ankylosaurs
Four-legged, plant-eating dinosaurs that had heavily armored bodies and sometimes had massive clubs on the end of their tails. They include *Ankylosaurus* and *Euoplocephalus*.

Ceratopsians
Four-legged, plant-eating dinosaurs that often had beaks and horns. They include *Triceratops* and *Protoceratops*.

Coprolites
The fossilized remains of dinosaur dung.

Cretaceous period
A period in the Earth's history that lasted from 135 million years ago until the extinction of the dinosaurs, some 65 million years ago.

Dinosaurs
Taken from the Greek for "terrible, or fearfully great lizard," the term refers to a group of land-living reptiles that flourished between 225 million years ago and 65 million years ago when they became extinct.

DNA
Short for deoxyribonucleic acid, this is the recipe that cells use to build living organisms. It is stored in the cell's nucleus.

Embryos
The very early stages of a young animal before it has been born or has hatched.

Extinction
When a whole group or species of animals or plants dies out.

Fossils
The preserved remains of something that was once alive. They can be formed in a number of ways, including burial and the chemical change of the body parts into minerals.

Gondwana
The large and ancient southern continent that was made up of what is now South America, Africa, India, Antarctica, and Australia.

Gymnosperms
A group of plants that do not produce flowers. The last remaining example of these once widespread plants is the gingko.

Hadrosaurs
Plant-eating dinosaurs that often had duckbill-shaped mouths and a crest on the top of their heads. They include *Edmotosaurus* and *Maiasaura*.

Timeline

Massopondylus

Syntarsus

Pterosaur

PERMIAN	TRIASSIC	JURASSIC
290 MYA	245 MYA	225 MYA

Hibernation
During winter, many animals hibernate to conserve energy through the cold months. This involves slowing down the body's processes and spending the time in a sleeplike state.

Ichthyosaurs
A group of sea-living reptiles from the age of the dinosaurs. These swimming animals had very streamlined, fish-shaped bodies.

Jurassic period
A period in the Earth's history that lasted from 200 million years ago to 135 million years ago.

Laurasia
The large and ancient northern continent that was made up of what is now North America, Europe, and Asia.

Migration
A movement from one place to another. Animals generally migrate to avoid the cold of winter or to search for food.

Paleoichnology
The study of dinosaur footprints.

Paleontologists
People who study fossils.

Permian Period
A period in the Earth's history, lasting from 290 million years ago to 245 million years ago.

Plesiosaurs
Although not actually dinosaurs, these flesh-eating sea creatures were around at the same time.

Pterosaurs
Flying reptiles from the dinosaur era. They were distantly related to dinosaurs.

Sauropods
Large, plant-eating, four-legged dinosaurs. They included *Seismosaurus* and *Diplodocus*.

Tertiary period
A period in the Earth's history that lasted from 65 million years ago to 1.8 million years ago.

Tethys Sea
A body of water that separated Laurasia and Gondwana.

Therizinosaurs
Plant-eating dinosaurs with long arms and huge claws. They include *Alxasaurus* and *Therizinosaurus*.

Theropods
A range of hunting dinosaurs that usually stood on two legs. They include *Tyrannosaurus* and *Eoraptor*.

Titanosaurs
Very large sauropods.

Triassic Period
A period in the Earth's history that lasted from 245 million years ago to 200 million years ago. The dinosaurs first appeared toward the end of this period.

Tyrannosaurs
Large, two-legged, flesh-eating dinosaurs. They include *Tyrannosaurus* and *Albertosaurus*.

Ultrasauros
Confuciusornis
Afrovenator
Triceratops
Extinction of the dinosaurs

CRETACEOUS

135 MYA

TERTIARY

65 MYA

Index

PHOTO CREDITS:

Abbreviations: *t-top, m-middle, b-bottom, r-right, l-left*
Pages 2, 6m & b, 8t, 9tl, 13, 14, 17, 19t & 29tr – Frank Spooner Pictures. 4t & m, 10t, 12, 15 both, 20, 27, 28m & 29tl – Science Photo Library. 5m, 7, 18-19, 19b, 22t, 23b & 24 – The Natural History Museum, London. 6t – Amblin/Universal (courtesy Kobal). 8bl – Dr Michael Benton, Bristol University. 9tr – Dr David Unwin, Bristol University. 8br, 9bl, 21b & 25 – Roger Vlitos. 10b, 16, 28t & b – Rex Features. 26 – Robert Harding Picture Library.

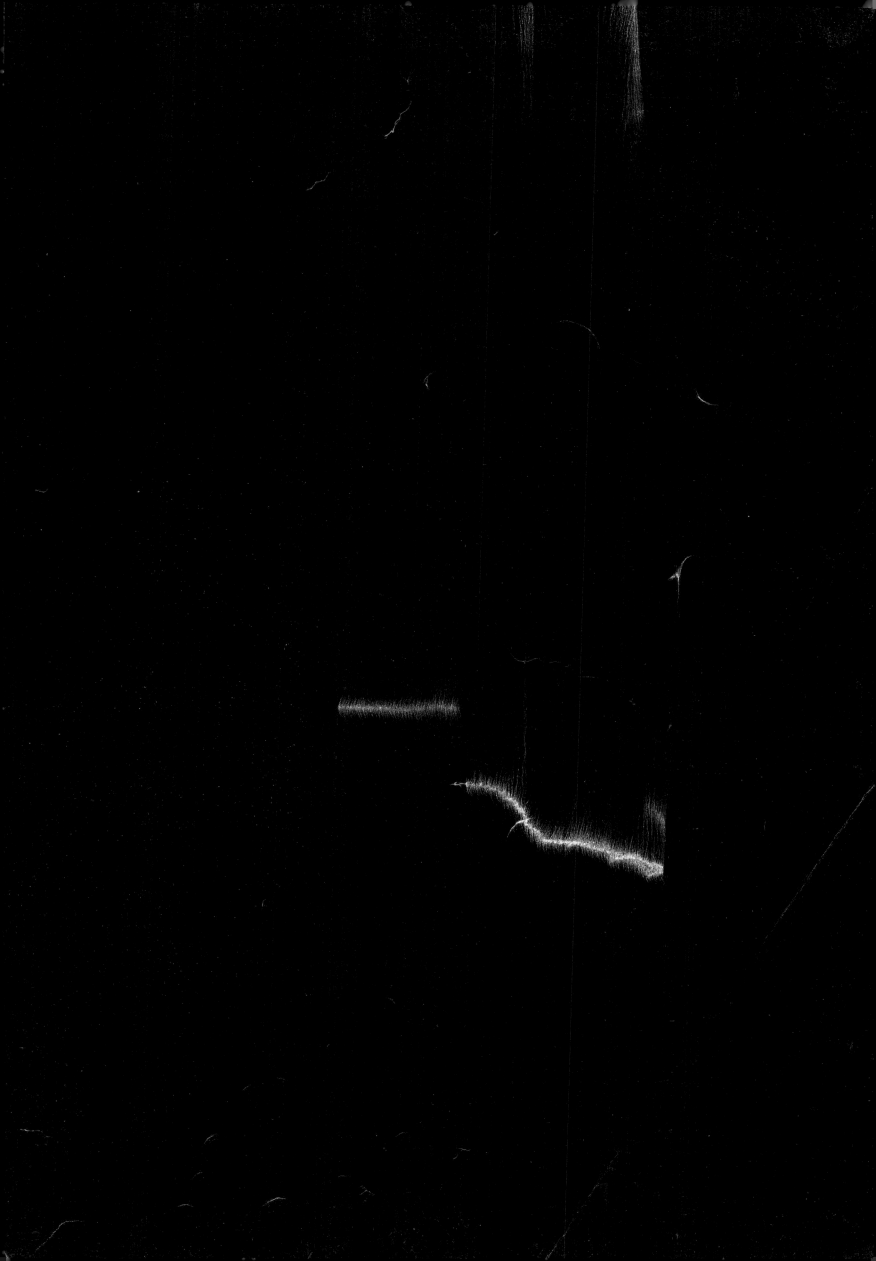